Apple Watch (2018 Edition) User Guide for Complete Beginners

Master Your Apple Watch in 60 minutes

Table of Contents

Introduction

The Apple Watch 2018 is one of the most advanced smartwatches on the market. Since its launch, ordinary people have gone wild and have been flocking to Apple stores across the nation to get their hands on this beast. What makes the Apple smartwatch so desirable among technology enthusiasts are its stunning looks and compelling features.

The modern-day Apple smartwatch comes loaded with an array of striking features. In simpler words, it is capable of making lives more comfortable and mobile. The smartwatch features excellent connectivity for the owner, compelling looks, and smartphone app compatibility. If a person is interested in owning a smartwatch, which provides them with seamless connectivity and compelling features, the Apple smartwatch is among the best options available.

The learning curve can be inherently steep, especially for the person that is not acquainted with former variants of the same. This e-book has been written to provide its readers with all the essential information about operating the smartwatch. This e-book provides a comprehensive insight into the connectivity features, customization features, and other compelling aspects of the device.

What Does the Apple-Watch Do?

One of the most common questions that arise in the minds of the people owning the Apple smartwatch for the first time is what the device is all about. Well, primarily it allows the owner to read emails, text messages, and receive calls. However, it is not just a device meant to serve the fundamentals. The features of the Apple smartwatch are far more intense than what meets the eye.

The Apple Watch serves as a fitness tracker for the owner. For people that are enthusiastic about sports, the smartwatch can be envisioned as a sports watch as well. The "wrist notification" feature ensures that a person does not have to carry their iPhone everywhere because the Apple smartwatch can be connected and synchronized with the owner's iPhone.

The interface has "Siri" (IOS virtual assistant) integrated to it which allows the user to set alarms, read emails, schedule appointments, navigate through GPS, set reminders, and much more.

The feature-packed device also possesses access to dedicated apps which include the likes of traffic notifications, navigation, and much more. With the launch of the "watchOS 4" for the Apple smartwatch, a large number of significant features have been revamped. The user can experience advanced heart-rate monitoring, metrics, pulse monitoring, newly designed watch faces, and health-hazard alarms.

The health-hazard alarm has been integrated to especially monitor irregular heartbeat, a drop in pulse, and other dangerous health symptoms. The probability of "watchOS 5" hitting the markets soon further ensures that the existing features will witness more enhancements.

Chapter 1: Setting up Your Apple Watch for the First Time

Once you have bought the Apple Watch, you will need to set it up. The process for setting up an Apple watch is relatively unchanged and straightforward for most of its variants. Whether it is an Apple Watch series 1 or series 2, the process is relatively comparable. The Apple Watch needs to be envisioned as a personalized amenity/electronic device. It is therefore essential for you to customize the features to your taste.

Connecting the Device to your

iPhone

The most fundamental part of setting up the Apple Watch is connecting it to the iPhone. It is essential for you to ensure that your iPhone is updated to the latest IOS version available for the device. For the procedure, you will require a stable internet connection, preferably a Wi-Fi network with quality internet speed. You will also need to ensure that the Bluetooth on the iPhone is activated. After you have assured all the aspects mentioned above, start your Apple Watch.

You will need to ensure that the iPhone variant you are using is an iPhone 5S or higher. You can start your Apple Watch by holding the side button, and it should boot automatically. Go to Apple Watch app on your iPhone and select the option asking you to pair a new Apple Watch. Following that, hold the Apple Watch within the camera viewfinder of the iPhone for further calibration.

A certain number of steps will follow which will prompt you to choose your desired language, watch orientation, (for left-handed people) and smartwatch passcode. After you have completed these steps, the basics of pairing the device with your iPhone and setting it up have been done.

Signing In to your Apple ID

To sign in to your Apple Watch and start using its features, you will require your Apple ID. Once you have signed in using the Apple ID, it is explicitly linked to your device and is going to stay that way unless you decide to have it manually unpaired. It is a significant aspect to enhance device security since it ensures that nobody except for you can access your device.

Setting Up the Passcode for the Apple Watch

The next thing that you will need to do is set up a passcode for your Apple Watch. This step isn't mandatory for all Apple devices, but it is an essential step if you are planning to use "Apple Pay" in the future. One of the positive aspects about the passcode is the fact that it does not have to enter every time you are accessing the smartwatch. The heart-rate monitor is capable of reading your pulse when the watch is placed on your wrist. This means that you will only need to unlock your Apple Watch once after you have worn it on your wrist.

The passcode in general needs to be long and you will need to create it on your iPhone, which has been paired with your Apple Watch. This will be done during the setup process after which the code needs to be entered on your Apple Watch. This feature also lets you unlock your iPhone along with your Apple Watch, but is optional. The basics of setting up your device have been completed.

Chapter 2: Installing Applications on Your Apple Watch

There are several standalone apps featured on the Apple Watch, but most of these applications are extended from the ones available on the Apple iPhone. As a user, you will be allowed to install several apps which are supported by the Apple Watch. Note that most of these applications are predominantly extended versions of the applications available on the iPhone. The new apps on the platform are added automatically onto the interface.

The Apple Watch features automatic installation options which can be turned off if needed. This should be done if you are not willing to install all of the apps that are installed in your iPhone. To access the feature, you will need to deactivate "automatic installation" from within the Apple Watch app on your iPhone. It is available on the first page where, if needed, you can manually opt to allow or disallow installation.

Turning Off Automatic App Installation

To turn off automatic app install:

- Start the Apple Watch app on your iPhone 5S or later variants

- Open the "My Watch" section by tapping on it

- Tap on the section which reads "General"

- You should see an "Automatic App Install" toggle that is lit green. This signifies that the feature is activated. Toggle the option, and the function is stopped.

Adding New Applications to your Apple Watch

To add new applications to the Apple Watch, follow these steps:

- Start the Apple Watch App on your iPhone

- Open the App Store

- Tap on the search button and in the search-query section, type in the name of the app that you wish to download

- Once the application has been found, tap on the "Get" option to initialize download of the app

- Click on the install option after the download has been completed.

Installing Pre-Downloaded Apps on your Apple Watch

It is possible for you to reinstall those apps that you have removed or downloaded across previous versions.

• Open the Apple Watch app on your iPhone

• Tap on the "My Watch" tab to open the next page

• A listing labeled "Available Apps" should be featured at the bottom of the page. Within the listing are those apps that you can restore or reinstall. Click on the "Install" option and initiate the process.

Chapter 3: Activity App

The activity app is among the core applications available to the user of the Apple Watch. The Apple Watch features an intriguing feature with which you will be able to monitor your activity using the activity tracker application and keep a note of your healthy lifestyle.

This is a free boost to those people that are into sports and lead an extremely active lifestyle. If you are getting started with a new lifestyle or perhaps a fitness training program, then this app will help you set goals and monitor your progress real-time.

The fitness tracking element helps you lead an active lifestyle and understand whether or not you are leading an active lifestyle. As a third-party app, there are several elements associated with the fitness tracker, but first, you need to get the app installed on your Apple Watch.

Getting the Activity App Initialized

The activity app which is available on the Apple Watch requires personalized information to assess and efficiently monitor your daily activity routine. The inputs made by you will be used by the interface of the application to estimate daily steps taken, calories burned over a long time, distance walked during the day, and much more. It is therefore essential for you to be accurate with your input details so that the most precise form of data can be received.

Now that you have the app installed on your Apple Watch, and have provided it with the requisite credentials, let's take a look at the most compelling aspects of the app.

• View your stats for the day

With the Apple Watch, you have the option to select open workout mode or set goals concerning time, calories burned, steps taken, the time limit for the exercise, and much more. Switching between the modes is very easy as you only need to swipe left or right on the screen. The advanced features also let you monitor your swimming stats. To access the functionality, you will need to accurately provide the details regarding the dimensions of the swimming pool.

The app metrics also take into account your heart rate to monitor the status. This is mainly taken into account during outdoor sports events like swimming, cycling, sprinting, and much more. The device also warns you if your heart rate gets too fast or starts to dip way below average.

- Customizing the metrics

The metrics provided by the Apple Watch interface tend to work pretty well, but at times, you may not like to view all the workout routines clustered together in the menu. Thus, you have the ability to customize them by yourself. To get the job done, all that you need to do is head over to the Apple Watch application on the paired iPhone. Following that, click on the "workout view" option, where you will be able to customize the metrics according to your preferences.

You will come across two primary options available to you, "Multiple Metric" and "Single Metric." They are each different in their own way. Mostly, the "Single Metric" will only show you single statistics and to view the others, spin the digital crown. On the other hand, "Multiple Metric" will provide you with various stats at the same time. In this case, note that the default metrics for different types of workout may not be the same.

For instance, the default metrics for cycling are duration, present speed, heart rate monitoring, and covered distance. On the other hand, the default metrics for outdoor walking or running include heart rate monitoring, range to be covered, the duration of the activity, and the active calories. These metrics are, however, independently customizable, which is an excellent thing if you long for more. Thus, you can add other parameters for cycling which include average speed, total and active calories, average distance, and much more.

• Running Auto Pause

"Running Auto Pause" is a great feature if you are into active lifestyle sessions, which include sprinting, jogging, or simply running for a long time. However, it is important that the device stops monitoring when you are in a neutral state or not in motion. The Apple Watch has been provided with this feature as well, which makes it simply one of a kind.

To access the feature, you will need to head for the companion app, access the workout app, and tap on the "Running Auto Pause" option. You are now all set to actively monitor your run without any hassle or multiple interruptions.

Chapter 4: Customization with Apple Watch Faces

The Apple Watch provides the user with some generous benefits in the domain of customization. One such tempting feature is the Apple Watch face customization. The faces are based on the nature of specific apps by which you will be able to access fundamental information without digging deep into the apps.

These watch faces cover most of the typical things that you might do during the day. For instance, there are watch faces for a workout, commuting, flying to international and domestic destinations, and much more. There are hundreds of watch-face combinations that you can make out. The following section provides you with a compilation of some of the most common and useful Apple Watch faces that you will need for your daily routine. You will also be able to customize them by integrating designs from several apps into one.

• The Runner Watch Face: If you are into an active lifestyle then this is the right watch face for you. In here you can integrate the number of steps taken, the heart-rate monitor, and efficient calorie burner stats as well. The rings on the watch face also allow you a holistic insight into the activities you have performed throughout the day.

• The Worker Watch Face: If you belong to the corporate world and have loads of responsibilities, then this is the must-have watch face in your arsenal. This watch face will allow you to keep track of your deadlines, scheduled meetings, and appointments at the same time. In case you need to make a note of something important, then try using this watch face as your personal sticky note.

• The Chef Watch Face: Are you into cooking? Well, in that case, you will need to be informed about the cooking ingredients, directions, and time required for the procedure. This watch face has the perfect compilation to let you keep track of the cooking essentials like the time, the ingredients, their measurements, and the entire process to be followed.

• The World Traveler Watch Face: If you are planning to visit several destinations throughout the world, then you can opt to use this watch face. It will allow you to keep track of flight timings, hotel reservations, train schedules, ticket prices, booking status, and cab rental status. You can consider it an all-in-one center for all the information you require.

• The Flyer Watch Face: If you are a frequent flyer and make use of airline services on an everyday basis, then this watch face will help you stay connected with flight status, schedule, and booking fundamentals. It will also allow you to see the temperature conditions and time on the world clock for the destination you are about to visit.

• The Adventure Seeker Watch Face: You can think of it as a fantastic combo for the people that undertake challenging tasks on a daily basis. You will be able to keep yourself updated with the weather conditions, track your activity for the day, and check out maps, trails, and much more while you are outdoors.

• The Sports and News Lover Watch Face: If you like to stay updated with the latest in sports and international news, then this combo is for you. The Apple News feature is intriguing. It compiles news from multiple resources and presents it to you as a whole unit. Staying updated with your surroundings has never been easier.

CHANGING WATCH FACES ON APPLE WATCH

To change the watch face on your Apple Watch, follow these steps:

• Press on the digital crown and navigate to your watch face

• Seek out the available clock faces of your choice by browsing through them. All you need to do is swipe left or right.

ADDING AN APPLE WATCH FACE TO YOUR LIST

If you wish to add a particular Apple Watch face to your list, then you need to follow the steps below:

• Take the connected iPhone and open the Apple Watch app

• Click on "Face Gallery" tab

- Select a watch face present on the list by just tapping on it

- After you have selected the watch face, tap on "Add" and the watch face will be automatically added to your Apple Watch interface.

ORGANIZING THE LIST OF APPLE WATCH FACES

To coordinate the list of customized Apple Watch faces, you should follow these steps:

- Open the Apple Watch app on the connected iPhone

- Select the "My Watch" tab, which can be seen on the screen

- On the right side of the watch face is an "Organize" button. Press the button.

- Drag the watch face to the desired position on the watch list.

After you have completed the steps, the new order of your Apple Watch faces will automatically appear on your Apple Watch.

Chapter 5: Amazing Apple Watch Tips and Tricks

The Apple Watch features an intriguing list of features and its own set of tricks. The operating system on the Apple Watch is among the most advanced on the market. It is because of this fact that the features you find in the Apple Watch are unlikely to be present in any other smartwatch of the same price segment.

Customization is among the most prolific benefits that you can enjoy with the Apple Watch. All features can be customized as per your needs. Here is a compilation of the tips and tricks to make your Apple Watch handier and more easily accessible.

- Organizing and using the App dock: One of the best features present in the Apple Watch is the fact that you can customize the watch dock through the Apple Watch app on your paired iPhone. The feature is similar to that of multitasking on the iPhone where you can recover the most frequently used apps or the apps that you have used recently. To customize the dock, click on the side button and then hold onto the desired app and tap "Keep in Dock."

- Tracking your sleep patterns: The Apple Watch does not provide you with a built-in sleep checking mode, but it makes use of third-party apps which provide the experience. There are several types of apps that are present in the IOS market which you can download and make track your sleep patterns. You can also make a fitness tracker watch face and customize it for instant access.

- Control music on the go: The Apple Watch also allows you to control music while on the move. This means that you will no longer need to use your iPhone to make changes to your playlist and music volume. With the integration of the watch-OS 4.3, you can now make changes and modify the music on the iPhone and the Home-Pod. You will be able to adjust the volume, skip music if you so desire, and select your playlist by using the Apple Watch. It is a simple and convenient solution for music lovers that do not like using their phone every time.

- Fancy bands are the next thing: Apple Watch bands are one of the most unusual ways to make your device look elegant and appealing. One of the best things happening out there is the fact that new bands are being launched now and then. In most cases, new colors are being integrated to suit the seasons. This makes the bands look appealing and coordinate with the season. These fancy bands will also help you match the Apple Watch with your wardrobe. In case you are heading out for a party or a casual meeting, these bands will help you complement your style and dress. There are several third-party options available as well, which can be taken into account if you do not want to shell out hefty bucks. It is fair to be warned though that these bands do not fit as well as Apple watch bands.

- Taking a screenshot on your Apple Watch: This is a great new feature which you can access from your Apple Watch. To take a screenshot, hold down the digital crown and the action button simultaneously. The action button can be found just below the digital crown. The images are saved in the default camera gallery on your iPhone. To access the feature, you will need to enable it first. To allow screenshots on the Apple Watch, head over to the companion app on the iPhone, open it, and tap "General." You will find an "enable screenshots" option which you will have to toggle to activate.

- Unlocking the watch from your iPhone: This feature can also be accessed during the initial startup process. However, if you have not done it as of yet, then there isn't any hassle since you can still unlock your Apple Watch from your iPhone without having to set a passcode. To perform the task mentioned above, open the companion app on the iPhone and toggle the "unlock with iPhone" feature.

Remember that you will need to wear the watch on your wrist to access this feature.

- Elevated heart rate notification: The Apple Watch is also a fitness tracker that will help you stay active and fit for the day. The heart rate monitoring on the Apple Watch has been integrated with a set of new features that warn you if your heart rate is higher or lower than usual. To enable the feature, you will need to activate it on the "heart rate" section present in the companion app on your iPhone. After you have activated the function, you will be asked to select a default threshold for heart rate monitoring which is between 100 to 150 beats per minute.

The app on the Apple Watch will trigger a warning once you have gone beyond the threshold or if you have been inactive for over ten minutes. The watch will also monitor your average heart rate conditions to assess whether the spike in heart rate is temporary or frequent.

- Unlock Mac from the Apple Watch: To access this feature, ensure that both the Apple Watch and the Mac are signed into the same iCloud account. Next, head over to your Mac and select system preferences. Following that select "Security & Privacy" and then click on the tab termed "General." Here, you will able to set the Apple Watch to unlock your Mac. It will be an added benefit if you can ensure two-factor authentication settings for your Mac. For this, head over to System Preferences, click on "iCloud," then select "Account Details" and then, finally, select "Security."

- Keeping a check on data usage: Your Apple Watch also warns you about data usage and allows you to monitor it on a real-time basis. To keep track of the data usage on your Apple Watch, go to your companion app and click on the cellular menu information to see the data. Here, you will be able to gain a comprehensive insight into the amount of data that you have used until now. Also, you will learn about the apps that are making use of data in real-time.

Chapter 6: Customizing Your Apple Watch Faces

Several customization features make the Apple Watch one of the best among other smartwatches of a similar price range. Customizing your Apple Watch is pretty fun, and it stretches beyond just setting the ideal watch face for the beast. There are several other features that you should check out.

Adding A Time Lapse Of Photo Face To The Apple Watch

You can change an Apple watch face to a time lapse. Isn't it great? Well, here is how you need to get started with it. You will also find a few time-lapse videos incorporated in the watch by default. These have been collected from various cultures and locations around the world.

- Start the watch face on your Apple Watch by double-pressing the digital crown.
- Hold the watch face by pressing on it, and the face-switching function should appear.
- Swipe to the left of the screen. This will allow you to select the time lapse option.
- Tap on the customize option if you wish to make any changes to the time lapse option.

- After you have done that, you need to turn the digital clock in a clockwise motion to browse the different locations for the time lapse. In most cases, it will be six locations.
- Tap the location which you want to select.

After you have completed the steps mentioned above, all you need to do is press the digital crown and the new watch face with time lapse will be set.

Setting a photo or photo album as the Apple Watch Face

The enhanced personalization experience on the Apple watch also allows you to set a photo or photo album as your default Apple Watch face.

- Press the digital crown on your Apple Watch and you should be on the home screen.
- Next, tap on the "Photo App."
- After you have done that, select the photo you wish to have on the watch face.
- Hold the photo by pressing firmly over it. After a while, the option to create a new watch

face should automatically appear on the screen.

You can also set a photo album as your default watch face. The process is straightforward and has been explained below:

- Open the Apple Watch app on your paired iPhone.
- Scroll down, and there you will see an option named "Photos." Tap on that.
- Next, tap on "Synced Album."
- Now select an album to synchronize with the photo app on the Apple Watch.

- Following that, press the digital crown and start with the watch face from here.
- Hold the watch face firmly for a few seconds and the watch face switcher will appear before you.
- Swipe to the left of the screen and select the "photo album watch face."

The best thing about the photo album watch face is the fact that every time you awaken the device, a new photo will appear, making the watch look more refreshing and more customizable.

How Do You Delete An Apple Watch Face?

Now that you have learned the customization tricks mentioned above, you may want to make a dozen new watch faces. This might make things monotonous for you. It is time for you to choose the best ones and get rid of the ones which do not fit the curve.

If you do not like a particular watch face, then you can always delete it if you want to. The process to remove an Apple Watch face is simple and not rocket science. Look below.

- Double-press the digital crown if you are not at the Apple Watch home screen.

- Hold firmly on to the watch face and the watch face switcher should appear after some time.

- Swipe left or right to locate the particular watch face that you want to avoid.

- Now that you have located the watch face which you want to delete, swipe up on the watch face.

- The "delete" option should appear. Tap on it.

Now you are familiarized with most of the customization features that Apple Watch faces have in store for you. You are ready to go, so get started!

Changing the Monogram On Your Apple Watch

The monogram on the Apple Watch can also be customized as per your needs. Though the customization concerning this aspect tends to be a little bit limited, you can make use of much more than simply your initials. You are allowed to set up to four characters of your choice for the monochrome complications or functions. Monochrome complications are functions that are meant to show measurement features other than time. These are displayed on the watch face as well. However, the sad news is that you are not allowed to make use of an emoji, but you can surely make use of the Apple symbol.

Changing the Monogram

- Start the Apple Watch App on your iPhone.
- Tap on My Watch.
- Tap on the clock, followed by the monogram.
- Here, you can enter your desired new monogram. You may find the default initials of the watch owner's name already present here. You can change these if you like.

- Tap on the return option at the bottom right of the keyboard.

After the steps mentioned above have been completed, the synchronization of the new monogram will initiate and finish within a short time.

To set the Apple symbol as your monogram, all you need to do is copy the logo onto the clipboard and paste it in the box where the default monogram was written. The entire detailed process is listed below.

- Copy the Apple symbol onto the clipboard when you are about to edit the monogram.
- Paste the symbol in the text box to edit the default monogram.

- Tap on return.

- On the Apple Watch, change the clock face to color by hitting the customize tab.

- Finally, change the original monogram function or complication to newly created one.

Chapter 7: The Fundamentals of Customization Settings

The settings on the Apple Watch can be further customized to suit your taste. You can name and rename your device or customize the notifications on your Apple Watch. The default weather application, world clock, and stock market are some of the fundamental features which you can customize to your taste.

Renaming your Apple Watch

You can now customize the identity of your device by renaming it. If you like your device, then you will love to provide it with a unique name of its own. It needs to have its own identity.

- Get the paired iPhone and open the Apple Watch app.
- Go to "General," followed by "About."
- Tap on the "Name" section and enter the new name that you want to give your device.

Customizing Mail, Calendar, Messaging, and other Notifications on your Apple Watch

There are specific built-in apps for Apple which can be tailored when they are downloaded onto the Apple Watch. The notifications can also be customized in such a way that you are alerted by a few apps which you prefer while keeping the others at bay. This feature isn't available with every app, but it does help in ensuring that unnecessary notifications do not bug you.

Customizing Activity Notifications

You can tailor the activity notifications. All you need to do is follow these steps.

- Launch the Apple Watch app on the paired iPhone device
- Head over to the "Notifications" area

- Tap on the option named "Activity."

Here, you can toggle the activity alerts for certain aspects like weekly stats, goals, weekly and monthly achievements, weekly summary reports, and much more.

Customizing The Calendar Notification

- Start the Apple Watch app on the paired iPhone device
- Tap on the notifications option, followed by "Calendar"
- Next, tap on "Custom."

The calendar notifications can be toggled on or off for many aspects including the upcoming events, exclusive parties, invitations, associations, official meetings, informal meetings and much more.

Customizing The Mail Notification

- Start the Apple Watch app on the paired iPhone device
- Tap on the notifications option, followed by "Mail"
- Next, tap on "Custom."

The mail alerts can be toggled on or off for mail alerts and mail notifications.

Customizing The Message Notifications

- Start the Apple Watch app on the paired iPhone device
- Tap on the notifications option
- Following the notifications, tap on "Messages"
- Next, tap on "Custom."

For messages, the alerts can be set to repeat never, once, twice, three times, five times, or even ten times.

Customizing The Phone Notifications

- Start the Apple Watch app on the paired iPhone device

- Tap on the notifications option
- Following the notifications, tap on "Phone"
- Next, tap on "Custom."

Customizing Reminder Notifications

- Start the Apple Watch app on the paired iPhone device
- Tap on the notifications option
- Following the notifications, tap on "Reminders"
- Next, tap on "Custom."

Chapter 8: Setting Default Weather, Stocks, and World Clock

The clock face of the Apple Watch is a great place to grab most of the essential information at a single glance. You can customize it to your needs, but specific features can be a bit tough to fathom. If you wish to customize the settings for your weather, then here is a guide on how to do it.

These steps will ensure that your Apple Watch face conveys you with all of the information that you need for now.

Setting Default Weather Location on Apple Watch

The Apple Watch and iPhone works in sync to provide you with weather updates and weather trends in your area. The first thing that you need to do is set up some specific weather options within the weather option present in your paired iPhone device. Note that before proceeding with the steps, you need to have the desired locations set up in the weather app currently on the paired iPhone device.

- Start the Apple Watch app on the paired iPhone device

- Tap on the "My Watch" option present at the bottom
- Tap on "Weather"
- Tap on the option "Default City."

You will see a list of current locations that are set up on the paired iPhone device. From this list, you can select any location and tap on it. To change the list of weather locations, you will have to make changes through the weather app on the paired iPhone device.

Setting Default Stock on Apple Watch

The Apple Watch is also capable of showing you real-time stock market updates. To make the setup, tap the "list of preferred stocks" saved on the paired iPhone device in the "Stocks" section.

- Launch the Apple Watch app on the paired iPhone device
- Tap the "My Watch" option present at the bottom of the screen
- Tap on "Stocks"
- A set of complications will be made available to you. These complications will include current pricing, market deviation, point change, percentage change, and market cap for the stocks. You will have

to choose amidst these complications.

- In the final step, tap on the "Default Stocks" option to create a list of the most popular or viewed stocks on the screen.

Setting the Default World Clock on Apple Watch

The Apple Watch makes use of data retrieved from the paired iPhone device to provide you with data associated with the world clock. It is possible for you to customize the world clock to be shown in "glances" by using the clock app on the paired iPhone device. The world clock options can be easily displayed across the watch face. The steps to customize the world clock at a glance are as follows"

- Open the clock app on your iPhone (the one specifically paired with the Apple Watch) and select the "World Clock" option, which is at the bottom left of the screen.

- If the time you wish to be shown isn't being displayed, then click on the "plus (+)" button. It is in the upper right corner and is used to add a new clock.

- After you have located the time of the place you wish to be shown, click on "Edit," in the upper-left corner of the screen.

- The world clock time zone that you wish to be shown can be explicitly rearranged according to your preferred order. All you need to do is drag the world clock options by your needs, and your list will be set accordingly.

When you set the list of the times of various locations as per your need, you will also find the time zone of the respective places besides the current time there.

These interesting customizing features are further enhanced with the option to customize the dedicated apps as well.

Chapter 9: Customizing Apps on Apple Watch

Custom messages help to personalize your Apple Watch interface to a greater extent. The personalization features associated with custom messages add another dimension to user accountability.

The message response has been crafted for individuals that need to be on the run most of the time. At times you may not have the opportunity to craft a profoundly involved reply, and that is where shorter variations are required. The custom responses help to make this ordeal easier for you. The Apple watch has its very own set of custom responses integrated, but at the same time, you can also create new ones based on your needs.

Adding Custom Message Responses

- First, to open the Apple Watch app on the paired iPhone
- Second, scroll down and select the "Messages" app
- Tap on the section reading "Default Replies"
- Tap on the option reading "Add Reply."

Here, you can create a short message reply depending upon your needs.

Deleting Custom Message Responses from the Apple Watch

- In the paired iPhone device, open the Apple Watch app.
- Scroll down to the point where messages appear. Select it.
- Tap on the option named "Default Replies."
- Tap on the "Edit" button
- You will come across a "-" sign on the side of the replies. Tap on that sign for the answers that you wish to delete from the Apple Watch message responses.
- Tap on the delete option that appears next.

In this way, you can delete the custom message responses that you do not require.

Reorder Custom Message Responses

It is also possible to reorder the custom message responses on your Apple Watch by individual steps. It further adds to the customization experience. The process to do is as follows:

- On the paired iPhone device, open the Apple Watch app
- Scroll down the screen and select the option reading "Messages"

- Tap on the option reading "Default Replies"
- Next, tap on the options reading, "Edit"
- You will come across a symbol resembling three stacked lines on the messages. Tap and hold to them for the words that you would like to move.
- Next, drag the selected messages to the desired location on the list.

Thus, the notifications can be sorted as per your preference, giving you a better experience.

Chapter 10: Setting Up and Using Activity Sharing

This feature has been integrated for individuals that are enthusiastic about fitness and prefer their daily fitness routines to be in groups. For instance, if you have a team or group of friends that workout together, then this feature is going to help you a lot.

Essentially, the fitness tracker app helps you to set goals and achieve them. Real-time monitoring is another intriguing feature of this activity-based application. Sharing of the activity app helps in customizing the training experience with your friends and associates. Mostly when this feature is enabled, other people can view your stats and compare their developments with yours.

In this way, you will be able to keep track of how your group's progress and shortcomings. This will help you to gain motivation for working harder so that you compare your goals with others.

Stats showed when the activity progress is shared

A few specific stats are displayed when you share your activity progress. These include:

- The day's activity rings which include exercise, static motion, and movements
- The number of calories you burn throughout the day
- The minutes that you have been indulged in intense to moderate exercise
- The hours throughout the day where you have stayed idle
- The number of steps you have taken throughout the day and the goals that you have set for the day
- The distance you have traveled on foot for the day.

One of the best features of the Apple Watch is that it respects your privacy and never shares the more personalized form of information. Any data concerning health that is collected by the Apple Watch is not shared with your friends or group. The same goes for heart rate monitoring stats as well.

The same pattern is also followed for your friends. When you share data, you will be able to see the progress they have made in the same way they will see yours. Thus, any form of personal data concerning your friends will not be made visible to you as well.

Several third-party fitness tracking apps can be downloaded into the Apple Watch. It is recommended that

you choose the app based on what
you will need over a long time.

Chapter 11: Navigating with Watch OS

For beginners, browsing with Watch OS can be a challenge. With the passage of time, things do get more comfortable. For those on the lookout for easy tips and tricks for navigating through the Watch OS, the following section is sure to come in handy.

The Apple Watch may be a small device, but it has loads of features to offer. With the integration of the Watch OS, these features have been enhanced to a significant level. The Apple Watch is similar to iPhone X when it comes to functions. The features that are in common include lack of a home screen button and full-screen display. Despite this evident lack of buttons with the interface, both the devices have a striking resemblance in features and functionality.

The side button is among the best assets for the owners of the Apple Watch. The side button can be used to turn the device on and off. At the same time, it can also be used to navigate to the home screen, access the dock, and the emergency features.

To turn on the device, all that you need to do is hold the side button when the device is switched off. Similarly, to switch off the device, all that you need to do is hold the side button and when the switch-off slider appears, slide it, and the device will turn off automatically.

Disabling the Power-Saver Mode

The power-saver mode is automatically turned on when the power level in the watch automatically drops below a certain level. The device switches itself to a power-saving mode so that it can reduce the amount of power used to a significant degree. In this mode, you will be only able to see the time, and the watch cannot be restored back to full functionality until it is connected to a charger and set to charge.

The Watch OS also provides for a power-saver mode which can be used as an emergency resource. In case you want to heavily use the watch later, then you can reserve power by activating power-saver mode. In this way, your device stays active, while consuming significantly lower power. When the watch has been put in power -saver mode manually, it can be transferred back to normal usage mode by pressing and holding the side button for a couple of seconds.

Accessing Medical ID or SOS

The power screen layers the Apple Watch's features like Medical ID and SOS. To access them, press and hold the side button for a short time. Then swipe either Medical ID or SOS, depending upon your need. The action mentioned above will activate either feature. Note that the SOS feature should be used only in case of severe emergencies because it will alert the authorities automatically if it is activated.

Enabling SOS on the Apple Watch app present on the connected iPhone, you can access the feature by continually pressing and holding the side button present on the Apple Watch. This will automatically activate the SOS feature and alert the local authorities.

Accessing the Dock

The dock can be used to store the most frequently used apps, which can be located later on from any other interface. To access the dock, press the side button a single time, and it will allow you to return to the previous screen. Next, you will have to press the side switch one more time.

Activating Apple Pay using the side button

The side button can also be used to enable the Apple Pay app. The Apple Pay is a handy app for people that perform online transactions and like to pay digitally and in a cashless manner. Even in the absence of your iPhone, you will be able to make use of Apple Pay.

The Apple Watch makes use of skin contact and an unlocked watch to authorize any purchase or transaction. To access the functionality, double-press the side button, and this should activate the Apple Pay interface. Following that, tap the watch to the payment terminal at the retail store, etc.

Chapter 12: Making Proficient Use of the Digital Crown

The digital crown is one of the best assets available for navigation across the Apple Watch interface. It's a physical dial which can be spun to scroll through the interface. If you press and hold the digital crown, then some features can be activated as well.

Waking up your watch

To wake the watch display after it has been sleeping for a while, all that you need to do is press the digital crown for a brief period, and this will awaken the display of the Apple

Watch. This also saves you from the hassle of raising your wrist.

If you want to avoid the sudden awakening of the Apple Watch and want to take the matter slowly and subtly, then you can scroll up in the display over the digital crown that will show the time and other functions on the watch face slowly without instant brightness. This feature comes in handy when you are mainly in some dark place where you need to quickly glance at the features without disturbing others near you, for example in a movie theater.

Using Time Travel on the Apple Watch

There are several instances where watch faces tend to stay active simultaneously. Scrolling down the digital crown will activate the time travel feature on the Apple Watch. This feature allows you to virtually travel through your schedule to view the appointments that you have or had throughout the day. It also lets you see the entire events of the day which include the steps you have taken, the calories you have burned, or the amount of exercise you have done. It also allows you to see the pending time for electricity charging, car charging, and another similar kinds of functions.

The motion of the Time Travel feature on the astronomy face is particularly intriguing. The time travel feature makes the shadow of the Earth pass around the sun, replicating the movement of the clouds. It also reveals the city lighting at night.

If you switch over to a different view in the astronomy section, then the digital crown is set automatically to control different time periods. If you tap the moon, the time travel feature will spin automatically day by day and reveal the various phases of the moon during different periods throughout the month.

If you select the solar system, then you will be able to move day by day. The speed will increase if you swipe and spin the crown even faster. It will make the planets complete their revolution around the sun quicker and let you experience the movement of the planets smoothly.

- Kaleidoscope Feature: The Kaleidoscope feature allows you to create repetitive geometric patterns when you swipe the digital crown. It is a fascinating personalization feature to consider.

- Siri: The Siri watch face helps in amplifying the time travel feature on the Apple Watch. It helps in offering cards related to any upcoming appointments or suggestions at the same time. The digital crown present on this watch face allows you to swipe through the forthcoming cards, all-day schedules, next-up views, and views for the next day as well.

- Solar Face: If you plan to use the Time Travel feature on the Solar Face, then it will move the positions of the sun which will take you through each phase of the day. Thus, you will be able to see nighttime, dawn, dusk, twilight, sunset, solar midnight, solar noon, and much more.

Scroll to view using the digital crown

The up and down motion of the digital crown can also be used to scroll through the content that is present on the screen. There are many other interfaces as well where scrolling the digital crown also moves the material horizontally, rather than vertically. An excellent example for those above would be the "watch picker."

The feature can also be used to scroll in the Photos app where the digital crown allows you to zoom in and out of the photo. In case the apps are organized in grid view, you can make use of the watch crown to climb in or out of the application grid present on the screen.

Ending the workout lock

When you press lock during a workout, the smartwatch automatically goes into water-lock mode. This means that you will not be able to make use of the touch interface on the screen during your workout unless you have manually unlocked it. To access the feature, you can scroll the digital crown upwards until you have filled the "blue bubble" on the screen, after which the watch speaker will ping.

Scrolling to adjust the volume

The Apple Watch can also be used to remotely access your music volume while the audio is playing through your iPhone or even on the watch. All you have to do is open the "Now Playing" mod and, using the digital crown, adjust the volume of the track being played right then.

You need to scroll the digital crown either up or down based on whether you want to increase the volume or decrease the volume. This is also applicable if you are playing podcasts or any other form of audible media.

Going back home or switching between applications

The digital crown can be used to maneuver between the active watch faces or the full application list. A single press of the digital crown will bring you to the current watch face or the complete app list. The digital crown will also help you to return to the previous interface if you press it once. The application is quite similar to that of the home button present on the iPhone models (excluding iPhone X). Pressing the digital crown will help you get back to where you wish to be.

Double-pressing the digital crown twice in quick succession will allow you to skip the watch face and simultaneously switch between the active apps. For instance, if you have the music app open, then you can quickly move to another app by accessing the dock. All you need to do is double-press the digital crown. In case you have a single app open, then double-pressing the digital crown will make you switch between the active watch face and the currently opened application.

CHAPTER 13: Efficiently Using the Dock on the Apple Watch

The Apple Watch is among the best available devices on the market if you are inclined towards active interaction. For instance, when you lift the arm, tap on the device, or swipe across the digital crown, dynamic interactions take place. The dock on the Apple Watch helps to make the interactions fast and accurate so that the user has a great experience.

The dock on the Apple Watch can be accessed using the side button. After you have obtained this feature, you will get to see a vertically scrolled list which displays the shortcuts to the apps that have been recently accessed or are present on the favorites. You can also modify this option using the Apple Watch app present on the paired iPhone device.

The shortcuts serve other purposes as well. For instance, they display the latest information from all existing apps in case you wish to check out notifications related to some aspect of the app. You can make the use of these shortcuts to quickly view messages, stock updates, or anything else.

When you look at the "Recent" section, you will be able to see a list of up to ten apps that have been opened recently. When you look at the "Favorites," you will see those apps that you have saved in the Favorites section of the Apple Watch App. In case the number of apps is less than ten in the Favorites section, then the dock will show you other recently opened apps alongside the list.

The default settings on the WatchOS 4 are set to display the shortcuts for the ten most recent applications that have been opened. This feature can, however, be changed under the Apple Watch app. This will allow you to pick ten of your favorite apps to be integrated into the shortcut. The process to do so has been detailed below:

- Open the My Watch App on the paired iPhone device
- Open the "My Watch" tab
- Tap on the options reading as "Dock"
- Under the "Dock Ordering" section, "Favorites" is present. Tap on it.
- Tap on "Edit" to modify the list.

If you wish to return to your recent or active app, then you can also perform that efficiently since the list will be saved by default.

Using Dock to Switch between Apps Quickly

The process to quickly switch between active apps using the dock is as follows:

- First, press the start button present on the side of the Apple Watch.
- You can scroll using the digital crown or merely decide to swipe.
- Finally, tap on the application that you want to see.

If you do not wish to see the dock anymore, then hit the side button to return to the previous screen. You can also tap on the digital crown to return to the previous screen.

Adding, Rearranging and Removing Apps from Apple Watch Dock

It is not possible for you to simultaneously switch between Recent and Favorites, but it is still possible to rearrange the dock depending on your needs. Using the Apple Watch, you can decide to add, reorder, and even remove apps from the Apple Watch dock.

In case you have fewer than ten Favorite apps, you can also add the most recent applications to that list, as described below:

Adding Apps

You need to scroll to the top of the dock list and hover on the top portion. In this way, the card on the top will expand, and the Recent tab will appear. It should display a "Keep in Dock" option.

- Click on the "Keep in Dock" option.
- Using the Apple Watch app, you can also keep your selection of apps stored in the "Favorites" section.
- Start the Apple Watch app on the paired iPhone.
- Tap on the "My Watch" tab.
- Next, tap on the "Dock" option.

- You will be able to see the "Edit" option in the top-right corner of the screen.
- From here, scroll down and find a "Do Not Include" option. Tap the green "+" button, which will prompt you to add the application to the dock.

Note that here, you are limited to a maximum of ten applications only, and therefore you are not allowed to add more than ten.

Rearranging Applications

Rearranging applications on the dock of the Apple Watch is only limited to those applications that are installed in the paired iPhone device. Also note that you need to have the "Favorite" mode enabled to be able to access this feature.

The steps to rearrange the applications on the Apple Watch dock are listed below:

- Open the Apple Watch App on the paired iPhone device
- Next, select the "My Watch" tab
- On the next page, select the "Dock" option
- In the upper-right corner, you should see the "Edit" option. Click on that.
- In this step, you will need to get a hold of the "grab handles"

button, which are placed next to their respective applications. Once it is selected, rearrange the selected app within the list as per your preference.

- When you have got the application to the dedicated part of the listing, release the grab handle button, and this should place the application to its designated new position on the list.

- In the final step, press "Done" in the upper-right corner of the screen.

Removing Applications from the Dock

Removing applications from the Apple Watch dock is easy and can be done using the paired iPhone device or the Apple Watch.

The process to remove the applications by the Apple Watch is as follows:

- Press the side button present on the Apple Watch, and this should open the "Dock" for you.
- Next, swipe or scroll along the screen to track the application that you wish to be removed.

- Swipe left and this will reveal the "Remove" tab for the designated application.
- Finally, tap on the "Remove" button and confirm the action.

The steps to the actions mentioned above in the paired iPhone device have been listed below.

- Open the "Apple Watch App" on the paired iPhone device
- Next, select the tab reading "My Watch"
- The "Dock" option will appear. Tap on it.
- In the upper-right corner of the next page, you will find the "Edit" tab. Click on it.

- The red "-" button will appear. Select it.
- Finally, tap on the "Remove Confirmation" button and the application will be removed from the dock of the Apple Watch.

Both of these processes are relatively easy and take very little time to complete for people that have access to their paired iPhone device or even the Apple Watch.

CHAPTER 14: Setting up and using Apple Pay

Apple Pay comes in handy for those people that need to make online purchases and wish to go cashless. It allows the user to make in-app purchases and in-store purchases with the device. While Apple Pay will enable you to make purchases using your iPhone or iPad, it can also be used on the Apple Watch. However, it is essential for you to install the Apple Watch on the paired iPhone device at first.

Once you have successfully installed the Apple Pay app on the paired iPhone device, the next thing you need to do is set up and add an iTunes payment card to Apple Pay on the Apple Watch. The steps have been listed below:

- Launch the Apple Watch app on the paired iPhone device.
- In the bottom navigation tray, tap on the "My Watch" option.
- Next, tap on the "Passbook and Apple Pay" option.
- In the next step, you will have to "Add Credit or Debit Card" for setting up the payment requisites.
- Tap on "Next" in the upper-right corner of the screen.
- Enter the security code for the iTunes card that you have.

- After entering the security code, tap on "Next," present in the upper-right corner of the screen.
- The terms and conditions page will appear; press "Agree."
- The iTunes card will immediately appear in the Apple Pay tab.

Adding more cards to Apple Pay

- Launch the Apple Watch app on the paired iPhone device.
- In the bottom navigation tray, tap on the "My Watch" option.
- Next, tap on the "Passbook and Apple Pay" option.

- In the next step, you will have to "Add Credit or Debit Card" for setting up the payment requisites.
- Tap on "Next" in the upper-right corner of the screen.
- A yellow box will appear where you are required to scan your card and let the app read all the requisite information. If this process does not work for you, then you can also tap on the "Add Card Details Manually" option and provide your details that way.
- Next, fill in the required fields that cannot be done by the app. Verify that the details captured

by the app are correct for the card and tap on "Next" in the upper-right corner of the screen.

Following the process mentioned above, you will be able to add multiple cards for Apple Pay on the Apple Watch device. Make sure you are careful while setting up your payment details. Double check every step.

CHAPTER 15: 8 Tips to Be Productive With the Apple Watch

The Apple Watch is a modern-day marvel. It has astounding customization features, an easy-to-use interface, and loads of essential elements. While making use of the watch, specific tips can help you to maintain the watch better and enhance your user experience. Take a look at them below:

- Covering the screen to turn off the device: This is a fantastic feature associated with the Apple Watch. All that you need to do is cover the top of the watch screen with your palm and form a cup-like shape. The AI sensor will then automatically shut off the device for you.

- Swapping between watch face and frequently used applications: Here is a tip where you can swap between the watch face and commonly used apps by double-tapping on the digital crown.

- More natural scrolling: To scroll through your app feed more efficiently, try diagonally arranging the apps. This will help make the interface look classier and provide the display with a hierarchical structure.

- Optimizing the glances on the Apple Watch: Glances are great features for better accessibility and ease of use. Though the element might not sound enticing to you at the beginning, you will use them frequently. Arrange the app list in such a way that you have the most frequented third-party apps at the top.

- Swiping to dismiss notifications: At times, notifications can become quite irritating. To deny them easily, swipe down from the top of the Apple Watch screen. Yes, it's that easy.

- Customizing Notifications: To make the experience of your Apple Watch even better, try customizing notifications for specific apps. At times you will not want to be bugged by unnecessary notifications. For such a scenario you can mute the notifications of specific apps for a specified time. Upon completion of the designated period, the app will resume its notifications.

- Go for multiple Watchbands: Apple Watch bands are expensive, and therefore it might not be possible for you to have a significant stock. You can, however, opt for third-party bands which do the work anyway. Having multiple watch bands at your disposal will ensure that you are prepared for almost any kind of occasion.

- Setting up Apple Pay: Apple Pay is a great feature and can come in handy anywhere. Apple Pay allows you to make purchases in a cashless manner. It is therefore recommended that you have Apple Pay set up on the Apple Watch. This will also ensure that you do not have to go through the hassle of taking out your iPhone to make a payment. All you have to do is make use of the smartwatch present on your wrist.

In general, the Apple Watch is an excellent asset for people who like smartwatches with loads of functionality. It will help to make things easier, faster, and more customizable for you than any other device comparable to a smartwatch.

References

https://www.wareable.com/apple/apple-watch-super-guide-the-missing-manual-001

https://www.imore.com/apple-watch-beginners-guide

49629851R00076

Made in the USA
Columbia, SC
25 January 2019